Australia

What Went Right?
What Went Wrong?

Australia

What Went Right?
What Went Wrong?

Anthony G. Percy

Connor Court Publishing

Published in 2022 by Connor Court Publishing Pty Ltd

Copyright © Anthony G Percy

All rights reserved. No part of this book may be reproduced or transmitted in any form or by any means, electronic or mechanical, including photo copying, recording or by any information storage and retrieval system, without prior permission in writing from the publisher.

Connor Court Publishing Pty Ltd
PO Box 7257
Redland Bay QLD 4165
sales@connorcourt.com
www.connorcourt.com
Phone 0497-900-685

Printed in Australia

ISBN: 9781922815248

Front cover design: Maria Giordano

The Weatherboard Falls, Blue Mountains, 1876, J. H. CARSE, Public Domain.

*This book is dedicated to
John Anthony Percy and
Joan Mary Percy*

Foreword

Chris Uhlmann

"Give me a place to stand, and a lever long enough, and I will move the world."

The first words of the boast by the Greek mathematician Archimedes are key, because no one can move the world without knowing where to plant their feet.

In the intellectual world, French philosopher René Descartes famously subjected everything he believed to radical doubt to try and find a shard of thought that was certain. He found Cogito, ergo sum: "I think, therefore I am". On that foundation he built his philosophy.

Nations need strong foundations if they are to endure, and rediscovering them is the purpose of this monograph by Fr Anthony Percy. Resting on the work of David Kemp's five volume political history, he goes in search of the liberal intellectual roots of Australia's democracy and asks what went right and what went wrong. He shows that, by any reasonable measure, the last 120-odd years prove the roots of this nation are strong.

He does not shrink from hard truths – the Original Sin of colonisation is dispossession, the White Australia Policy is another stain. Intellectual ideals are routinely breached in the real world. It is a reason to return to them, not reject them.

This work is timely and important because we live in an era where some would deconstruct everything. They appear determined to look back in anger at our past, tear down every physical statue and lift up every intellectual flagstone to erase what they believe to be an irredeemably racist, patriarchal colonial project.

And then what? If we are now able to confront our failures and seek redress, doesn't that stand as testament to the strength of our democracy? Liberal thinking led us to this enlightenment. Discarding that is not just misguided, it's dangerous.

In a *Man for All Seasons* the character of Thomas More is not pitched as a saint but a man of conscience with a deep faith in both God and English law.

More's son-in-law, William Roper, is a Lutheran zealot. In a seminal scene in the play, More's family is appalled by an encounter with Richard Rich, a man they rightly see as evil and whose perjury will lead to More's execution. They urge More to arrest him.

More says Rich should go free even if "he was the Devil himself, until he broke the law".

Roper: "So now you give the Devil the benefit of the law."

More: "Yes! What would you do? Cut a great road through the law to get after the Devil?"

Roper: "Yes, I'd cut down every law in England to do that!"

More: "Oh? And when the last law was down, and the Devil turned 'round on you, where would you hide, Roper, the laws all being flat? This country is planted thick with laws from coast to coast - man's laws, not God's - and if you cut them down d'you really think you could stand upright in the winds that would blow then? Yes I'd give the Devil the benefit of the law, for my own safety's sake."

Fierce winds are blowing in the world. There is a contest between autocracies and democracies for the way the world should be run. We can only endure if we do not tear ourselves apart internally.

Our land is built on laws aimed at ensuring fundamental human rights. That system is self-evidently better than the alternatives. If we are to survive as a liberal democracy for the next 100 years then we need to plant our feet on the foundation that has stood the test of time.

Prologue

This brief monograph is just that. It does not pretend to be comprehensive in the least.

It is the fruit of a three-month sabbatical. The Jews believed in the weekly rest called the *Sabbath.* Christians adopted the practice, but on a Sunday.

Eminently sensible, it is a time to stop, look back and so complete the week of work.

Longer periods of sabbatical became part of western culture. It enables a more interior time, not inactive, but less filled with the daily routine of life.

It was a grace being able to look at the subject matter of this work. Australia is one of the first truly modern countries. Living here is a gift and privilege.

A desire and passion was aroused within me about the history and culture of Australia.

It urged me to try and make it accessible to as wide a range of people as possible; after all, they are the 'polis' and they are able to preserve and enhance what has been bequeathed to us.

Introduction

Australia is unique.

It is geographically unique.

It is a continent, an island, a country, with neighbours close by.

Before the sea levels rose by approximately 150 metres around 20,000 years ago, you could walk, if you wanted to, from Tasmania to Papua New Guinea with minor interruption.

Indigenous Australians, the first immigrants to Australia, probably came from Africa, through India, around 65,000 years ago, wading across the archipelago.

They were stranded when the seas rose, but not prisoners, traversing the continent freely on their lonesome until the late 18th Century.

Captain Cook, who charted the east coast in 1770, wrote of the *First Nations Peoples:*

> *They may appear to some to be the most wretched people on earth, but in reality they are far more happier than we Europeans; being wholly unacquainted not only with the superfluous but the necessary conveniences so much sought after in*

Europe, they are happy in not knowing the use of them.

They live in a tranquillity which is not disturbed by the inequality of the condition (Cook's Diary, National Library of Australia).

It was a good beginning, but the 'clash of civilisations' was inevitable, brutal and violent. The encounter has been described as akin to a 'tsunami' for Aboriginals.

It was to be an encounter between the oldest culture in the world with the new world of science, of political and cultural liberalism, and of society erupting with material wealth, facilitated by the Industrial Revolution.

Australia is politically and culturally unique.

The second migration to the country involved the arrival of 11 boats in 1788 – loaded with some 750 convicts. Imagine it. Everything from scratch.

How is it that by the middle of the 19th Century, Australia had the world's most highly productive agricultural sector, the most advanced market system on earth, accompanied by wealth distribution better than any other nation, enabling the world's highest per capita income?

In such a short space of time, a free press existed, humane reform of the convict system and its subsequent abolition was achieved, self-government of significance emerged from the executive rule of Governors, separation of Church and State was pursued and honoured, the right of association was upheld – paving the way for a plethora of intermediary community bodies and groupings, including trade unions – a system of law was embedded that made land available to the masses and provided protection against violence, trespass and fraud.

Despite political, economic and cultural struggles and 'slippages' along the way, to this day Australia remains remarkable.

Think life expectancy, educational opportunities – both public and private – freedom and diversity in social and religious life, public and private medical health care with universal reach, political and civil stability through rule of law, abundant leisure time, material wealth – fifty-sixth in world population, yet twelfth largest economy (2015), having, remarkably, the fifth biggest pension fund in the world.

Is it luck? Is it divine predilection? Is it the result of human intent? David Kemp's five volume political history of Australia offers clues.

Formerly Professor of Politics at Monash University and minister in Howard's Government, Fellow of the Australia and New Zealand School of Government, Kemp has bequeathed a gift that will take primary, secondary and tertiary educators years to *unwrap* and *repackage* in various forms.

The Land of Dreams: How Australians Won Their Freedom (1788-1860) is volume one of the series and was published in 2018.

Kemp argues compellingly that the founders of the country rejected *Aristocratic Conservatism,* with its emphasis on a few privileged people having access to wealth (land and property) and power (governance).

Likewise, the leaders in the early years of the second migration rejected *Utopian Socialism* with its emphasis on the abolition of private property. How can poverty be alleviated if there is no incentive for industriousness and ingenuity, whereby initiative is honoured and rewarded?

Rather, Governors, Immigrants, Emancipists, Convicts, Australian-born citizens, embraced the new liberal forms of thought, expressed in politics, economics and culture which arose in the 18th and 19th Centuries.

It meant that Australia pursued a free and fair country in many aspects of life, but with a few unfortunate and notable exceptions.

A society based on privilege and class was rejected. A society based on the collectivisation of property was rejected.

Importantly, we rejected the 'inevitability of violent class struggle' theorised and proposed by Marx and Engels, ensuring peace and social harmony for the nation's inhabitants.

Rather, we wanted a society that traversed the social and political middle ground, one that would be free and egalitarian. With the support of those with varied political persuasions, it was achieved.

It is of enormous historical significance that Australia rejected slavery from its very beginnings, despite the fact that many countries – including the United Kingdom and the United States of America – had walked that dreaded path.

It is testimony to our Christian heritage – whether we like it or not – that William Wilberforce (1759-1833) was able to have such a powerful influence on those who journeyed to the *Great Southern Land.* Kemp maintains that:

> *Arthur Phillip carried with him in his instructions the substance of Wilberforce's implacable Evangelical opposition to slavery, and all succeeding governors, and the representative governments that followed from mid-century [19th], maintained this principle and its underlying value (Kemp, Land of Dreams, 15).*

It is testimony, too, that the liberal forms of thought that were unleashed in the 18th and 19th Centuries included what became known as *Humanitarianism.*

Australia was to be one of the first truly modern countries – a 'political experiment' if you like – where liberty and justice would be given a chance.

It is true that the dignity and value of each human being and the fundamental freedom of each human person is not a new idea.

Jesus of Nazareth proclaimed it and lived it. The Churches have tried to emulate him and have had mixed and varied success down the ages. Other religions and philosophies have attempted it. The *Universal Declaration of Human Rights (1946)* is based on it and draws out implications for behaviour.

But the most influential thinkers of the 18th and 19th Century applied the principle to politics, economics and culture in the new world emerging with the Industrial Revolution. It was an attempt to base an entire polis on the principle, not just the pursuit of intermediary groups.

Adam Smith (1723-1790), Jeremy Bentham (1748-1832), Mary Wollstonecraft (1759-1797), John Stuart Mill (1806-1873) and Wilberforce, to name a few, had extraordinary impact, providing intellectual rigour to the project.

Nothing is perfect; never was, is or will be. Utopians think otherwise, but they forget that the word actually means 'no place.'

History reveals that there is *'Blood on the Wattle:'*

> *Despite official policies based on the rights and humanity of native peoples, the tsunami of British settlement, particularly on the frontiers, involved a huge human cost in the abuse of and violence against the aboriginal peoples with whom it came into contact.*

> *Many of the settlers themselves did not share the moral codes of the leaders of their governments, and the governments, although liberal in principle, were unable for many decades to control the forces they had unleashed (Kemp, Land of Dreams, 14).*

There are unfortunate and notable exceptions to our pursuit of a free and fair country. Treatment of Australia's Indigenous peoples, the exclusion of Chinese people after initial engagement, the near enslavement of Polynesian Peoples, the *White Australia Policy,* developed almost simultaneously with Federation. We have our scars. No nation is without them.

But to this day, few have a *political, economic and cultural pulse* as strong as Australia's. How was this achieved? How do we maintain and promote it?

Chapter 1 uncovers the seeds of modernity sown in the ancient world and in the *Middle Ages*. Whose 'shoulders are we standing on?' Can we deepen our understanding of the origins of Australia as one of the first truly modern societies?

Chapter 2 begins with the *First Fleet* and asks, 'What happened and why?' Ideas become reality with men and women of desire and practicality. The story of the governors of the Colony of New South Wales is fascinating, revealing the 'what' and the 'why.'

Chapter 3 asks, 'What went right and what went wrong?' Federation was achieved by 1901. The *Constitution of the Commonwealth of Australia* was the fruit of two conventions spanning the last decade of the 19th Century. It was a magnificent achievement. Despite mistakes and setbacks, the first hundred years since Federation have been fruitful.

The Conclusion asks, 'What will the next hundred years look like?' 'What challenges do we face?' 'Is there a paradigm that can help us to pursue a free and fair country in the 21st Century?'

I

History is our Witness

Chaos is the fallback position.

It is not usual for there to be 'peace in the polis.' Darkness, emptiness and chaos seem to be the 'natural state of play.'

History is our witness.

Reading Rodger Charles' detailed and compelling history of the interplay between Church and State *(Christian Social Witness 1998)* since the time of Christ confirms the insight. Indeed, the period of peace experienced since the Second World War is not only unusual but extraordinary. The world is normally at war.

Divine wisdom, as is its custom, confirms and enlightens human experience:

> *The earth was without form and void, and darkness was over the face of the deep (Genesis 1).*

Not content with the underlying disorder, we seek change and transformation for we are creative beings. Greek philosophers, men and women of reason, from the earliest times of considered and ordered thought have bequeathed us the cardinal virtues:

Prudence, Temperance, Justice, Fortitude, Piety.

The Christian world accepted and embraced the Greek paradigm because it was natural, reasonable. Full of common sense and validated by human experience, it complemented the theological virtues of faith, hope and love.

Cardinal is from the Latin and means 'hinge.' A door is next to useless without a hinge, unable to be opened and closed. A society of worth is only obtained when personally and collectively we 'open the door' to virtue and 'close the door' to vice:

> *Prudence, the ability to 'see' the truth of things, requires of us that we work with others, gathering wisdom from various fonts.*
>
> *Temperance is harmony and tries to enjoy the more sensual things of life with due order, closing the door to the ever-present temptation to pervert the beauty of sensuality, thereby delivering inner and outer harmony.*
>
> *Fear is a predominant emotion, entirely necessary in the face of danger and difficulty. Yet we are able to call upon our inner depths and let courage be aroused to face reality.*
>
> *Justice, that profoundly rich virtue which should not be compressed or restricted to social justice alone.*

What Went Right? What Went Wrong?

Justice is recognition that life is relationship. What do I owe you? What do you owe me? We are mutual beings and obligations arise, that when met with graciousness, ensure peace, harmony and fulfill our desire for happiness.

What do members of families owe each other? What do employers and employees owe each other, teachers and students, doctors and patients, lawyers and clients, governments and people, sellers and buyers?

Justice is profoundly important, since like the other cardinal virtues, it endeavours to help light emerge from darkness, fullness from emptiness, order from chaos.

From Aristotle and Plato, through the Stoics and Roman jurisprudence, and re-presented by various, not all, liberal thinkers of the 18th and 19th Centuries, the mantra has been and is: *'Peace is the fruit of justice.'*

When justice is *legislated* in law, defended by *judiciary,* relentlessly pursued and *executed* for each human being by governments and ordinary citizens too, peace is approached. Australia has experienced this political phenomenon for an extended period, but it is not common or to be presumed.

Being one of the first truly modern nations on the planet, Australia has benefited from the lessons of long and sometimes brutal struggles between nations, and between political and cultural groups within nation states, at different times and various epochs, the majority of whom were and still are searching for freedom and justice.

In The Beginning

Interpreting history is hazardous. Thomas Stransky cites Walter Raleigh (1552-1618) and Chou En-lai (1898-1976):

> *Any writer of modern history who treads too closely on the heels of events may get his or her teeth knocked out. And one ponders the calm reply of Chou En-lai when a European intellectual asked the premier of China what he thought of the eighteenth-century French Revolution: 'It's too early to tell' (Pius XII and the Second World War 1999).*

Trepidation is required, but not timidity, otherwise we forfeit reason and experience. The history of the modern world and the Christian Church is intimately interwoven. This cannot be denied or avoided.

Mention of it does not necessarily offer a defence of the interaction, but simply acknowledges historical reality. It would be impossible to understand where we find ourselves today, politically and culturally, if the beginning and subsequent journey travelled are not acknowledged and understood in some way.

If Christianity had been founded in the last couple of centuries, then undoubtedly the interaction with the State would be substantially different, perhaps preferred. But of course it began in an ancient, primitive society with its language, culture and customs, and political forms.

The Romans had entered the Holy Land in 63BC. The Roman Republic began 509BC, with elected magistrates replacing their monarchy. It lasted until 27BC, when an imperial monarchy arose, with Augustus ruling as Emperor until 14AD.

The second-century Empire flourished with emperors chosen on ability, not blood-line, but fifty years of anarchy followed in the third century with no less than twenty-three emperors occupying the seat of power.

Historians tell us that Diocletian (284-305AD) restored order, which included the persecution of Christians, just ahead of the Edict of Milan (313AD) which recognised Christianity and elevated its status in the empire. Incredibly, by 323AD all coins in the Empire carried Christian images.

The empire collapsed in the 5th and 6th Centuries, followed by a period known as the *Middle Ages* (590-1500AD), with three stages: 590-1050AD; 1050-1300AD; 1300-1500AD. It was this period of time that saw the closest alignment of Church and State.

The claim of Christians is unique in world history.

It is that the *Son of Man* – Jesus of Nazareth – is the *Son of God*. That he was conceived and born of a Virgin (6-4BC) named Mary, that he lived an ordinary life, including manual work, for some 30 years, exercised an extraordinary public ministry for just on three years, ending in disgrace (27AD).

That he was crucified as a criminal is not contested. Secular and sacred sources concur. That he rose from the dead to a 'new life' – known as resurrection, not resuscitation – is the further outstanding claim.

An empty tomb helps argue the point, and resurrection appearances, few in number to be sure, further embedded belief among the few followers of Jesus who became the Christ. Before long, as they grew in number quite rapidly, they were nicknamed 'Christians.'

The essential teaching of Jesus of Nazareth centres on love – love *received* from God and love *offered* to God and one's fellow human beings. For the early Christians, love became a way of life, so they often referred to their movement as the *Way*.

In the first three centuries Christians lived without recognition from the State, often under persecutions, sometimes suffering martyrdom – an act that originated from Jesus' own act of freely laying down his life, shunning violent resistance. It was the reason that they used and refashioned the Greek word *agape*. Jesus' love was more than familial or friendly love. It was a self-sacrificing love.

The martyrs were men and women, young and old, rich and poor. Martyrdom must surely have acted as a catalyst in helping thinkers – philosophers, theologians, historians, sociologists, psychologists, scientists, etc. – understand the essential nature of the freedom and truth of the human person.

How could one possibly offer oneself to the point of death? What anthropology underscored the motive? What they seemed to say in their death was, 'the logical conclusion of believing the truth is that you are prepared to die for it.'

Cicero and Seneca made their contributions, no doubt, but here something new was presenting and manifesting itself in human affairs, which seemed to transcend, not contradict, human reason.

As Charles notes, it certainly has given rise to the central tenet of Christian Catholic social teaching, namely that 'individual human beings are the *foundation,* the *cause* and the *end* of every social institution *(Christian Social Witness, 3).*

The claim of later Christians, those bearing the grace of being able to look back over 20 centuries of Christianity, is not that the Church has been singularly faithful to Christ or the tenet. Rather, the 'natural state of play,' the 'fallback position,' inevitably remerges down the centuries.

Indeed it motivated Pope John Paul II in the Year 2000 to set aside a *Day of Forgiveness,* whereby he asked pardon for an array of sins committed in the name of the Church in her 2,000 year history. It was a sobering act for those on the *Way,* but truth must out and when it does it liberates.

Besides martyrdom, another key symbol of Christianity in the first three centuries was love for the poor, having lasting impact upon Western society and more than likely being, if not the *cause,* then the *occasion* of modern forms of welfare. Christians took seriously the mysterious teaching of Jesus that he is present in the 'hungry, thirsty, stranger, naked, sick, prisoners' *(Matthew 25).*

Rodney Stark (*The Rise of Christianity 1996*) examines from a sociological, not theological, perspective the activity of the infant Christian community. How is it that a small marginal movement of Jews and Gentiles rose and developed so quickly? His twofold answer is a revelation itself.

Christians were noted for their practical charity, so much so, that when plagues and pandemics obliterated ancient societies, the proportion of Christians remaining was significantly greater than other groups. They were better at attending to the sick.

Death also opened the door to conversion. Post-pandemic life left fewer familial objectors to Baptism. Conversions grew in number.

Stark's research uncovered the significance of the Christian teaching on the indissolubility of marriage and associated moral practices. Christian men, in contrast to other men, were encouraged to be faithful to their wives. Christ's teaching, and Paul's symbolic explanation of it, were powerful agents of change.

Personal, marital and familial stability ensured, resulting in societal harmony. Over the ages, faithful and fruitful marriages contributed enormously to social solidity and peace, acting, as some social commentators and politicians have noted, as the most natural social welfare institution known to humanity.

The mantra began to be: *marriage is for family, family is*

for society.

At the time, we know that the Empire was experiencing unsustainably low marriage rates, causing emperors to issue decrees compelling men to marry. The initiative had little success, but imagine it.

The fact that infanticide and abortion were forbidden, enhanced Christian birth rates, as did the discouragement of contraceptive practices. Christians began to outpace other groups in the demographic stakes.

In contrast to some modern views, women in the ancient world felt liberated by these customs and teachings. Placing ourselves in the shoes of the women – especially Jewish – of those first centuries is not a bad idea.

From the time of Abraham (1850BC), a woman gained her dignity by being joined to a *circumcised* male in marriage. The Jews understood the marriage covenant to be a *participation* in the covenant with God himself, but also being its *mirror,* its reflection. Experiencing the love of husband and wife, of mum and dad, was instrumental in helping others, especially the children, experience the love of God.

But with Jesus, physical circumcision was no longer required. In fact, and of great importance, Baptism was now the *gateway* and *sign* of the covenant. It was the new circumcision.

Women no longer required the mediatorial role of men

to be one with their God. They simply needed to receive Baptism, gaining for them freedom with God, in and through Christ by waters of 'new life.'

Equal recognition in the community of faith followed naturally enough, demonstrating the fundamental equality of women with men in the early Christian communities. It certainly carried forth the radical attitude of Christ towards women, especially demonstrated by Luke's Gospel, the most mutual and complementary of all the Gospels. Men are called. Women are called. Luke places the narratives side by side. He does the same with the parables of Jesus. First a masculine image, then a feminine image for the Kingdom of God.

The wealth obtained by conquest eventually corrupted the Empire. It receded and collapsed (476AD). What was left?

It became apparent that the Church had at its disposal many of the administrative and social services that the State could easily rely upon to help facilitate stability during relentless Barbarian invasions. The Church, for instance, maintained the births and deaths registrar, provided hospices for the poor, aged and travelers, hospitals for the sick, education through monasteries and cathedral schools.

The Council of Nicea (325) approved facilities for pilgrims, the sick and poor. What became known as *xenodochia,* a house for the needy, was common. These houses catered for strangers, vulnerable women, sick, poor, travelers, the old, orphans.

The papacy, in particular, gained increasing temporal prominence. Pope Leo the Great's (440-461) repelling of the Huns is well known and symbolic. Beginning with Charlemagne in 800, Frankish Rulers were acknowledged by the Church as successors of the emperors of the Empire, symbolic of the intertwining of Church and State.

The Middle Ages – A Rip van Winkle Moment?

Were the Middle Ages a period of superstition and irrationality as Voltaire (1694-1778) claimed? Charles comments:

> *One hundred years ago 'everyone deplored the Middle Ages.' It was seen as a Rip van Winkle period from which Europe was awakened by the Renaissance and the Reformation (Christian Social Witness, 104).*

Voltaire with his genius and French wit convinced many. But did he 'tread too closely on the heels of the events and get his teeth knocked out'? He may well have – died without teeth, that is.

Whilst the closeness of Church and State in the Middle Age period may now present as undesirable, there is little doubt that it did provide societal stability at the time, and furthermore, helped sow the seeds of modernity. Charles asserts:

> *The truth is that the Middle Ages was an intensively*

> *creative time.*
>
> *In these years the ideas of Western civilisation on economics, society, politics and philosophy were being formed and many of the institutions of modern times had their beginnings (Christian Social Witness, 104).*

Think representative government, constitutional monarchy, trial by jury and the establishment of universities, with reason becoming a partner with faith in the search for truth.

As the Empire collapsed, some Christians withdrew from the city. St. Benedict (480-547) left Rome in disgust at the collapse of morality. It was not a protest like some who left for the African desert – St. Antony of Egypt (251-356) – a railing against the classical culture of the Greek and Roman worlds,' but rather a 'retreat' in search of a richer social and cooperative life.

Benedict was to develop not only a monastic rule that to this day persists, but a system of government, and a community life that influenced and helped transform Western ways and thoughts.

The ancient world understood manual work to be for slaves. Christ turned this attitude on its head with his 25 years of manual work in Nazareth. The Benedictine Rule stipulated the combination of intellectual work with manual work, meaning that the 'monk was the first intellectual to get dirt under his fingernails.'

White highlights this significant historical moment:

> *In antiquity learned men did not work, and workers were not learned. Consequently ancient science consisted mostly of observation and abstract thought. Experimental methods were rarely used (Dynamo and Virgin Reconsidered 1958, 188).*

The 'old artificial barrier between the empirical and the speculative' was lowered. The seed of the scientific method sown. Dougherty rams home the point. The combination of mind and hands brought immense benefits to society:

> *The disciplined and tireless labor of the monks brought back into cultivation the lands which had been deserted and depopulated during the age of the invasions.*
>
> *As John H. Newman beautifully described the period, 'by degrees the woody swamp became a hermitage, a religious house, a farm, an abbey, a village, a seminary, a school of learning and a city (Intellectuals with dirt under their fingernails 1982, 230).*

Dougherty documents the array of inventions that took place from the 7th to the 16th centuries, agrarian by nature. Proficiency in Arabic and Greek enabling advancement:

> *Astronomical advances, including determining the date of Easter, fixing latitude and determining true north, telling time with astrolabe. Treatises were developed for the preparation of pigments and other chemical substances.*

It seems clear that the encyclopaedias in the 13th Century contain accurate information about the compass, the calendar, chemistry and agriculture, all a reflection of a long tradition of monastic learning.

The Benedictines developed mines, saltworks, foundries and glassworks in Bohemia, Germany and Hungary. Advances in spinning and weaving, pulling and dying, in felt making, in the manufacturing of soap, in the making of barrels and tubs. The cultivation of rye, oats and hops in the north is thought to be the result of monastic initiative.

The modern horse collar, the tandem harness and the horseshoe had far-reaching effects on the economy in Western Europe. These in the late 9th and early 10th centuries, greatly enhancing the effectiveness of animal power (Dynamo and Virgin Reconsidered, 233-234).

The constitutions of religious orders, including the Benedictines, with their representative style and procedures for governance, should not be overstated, but neither underestimated.

Arbitrary rule, failures in France and inordinate tax levies placed King John in hot water and led to the *Magna Carta (1215)*. Not exactly revolutionary, it did bind the King to the observance of established custom, no longer able to sideline the law:

The value of the Charter is that it stands as the first firm step towards formal representative government and then its democratic form (Christian Social Witness, 176).

The restriction on arbitrary rule and representation and democratic form in some mode, was and is, characteristic of the constitutions of the religious orders. For example, the Benedictines (6th Century), Augustinians (11th Century), Franciscans and Dominicans (13th Century).

Was it possible, given the monasteries profound influence, that their representative governance had no influence on the thinking and customs of the time?

Feudalism reigned from the 9th to 15th Centuries. With Charlemagne's empire imploding, anarchy arose in the 9th and 10th Centuries, with Church corruption replete. Not happy days.

Various reform movements arose including the Augustinians, who were 'most prolific,' and the Gregorian reforms of the 11th and 12th Centuries, insisting upon a better education for clergy – one important element in expunging Church corruption.

And then the universities arose – and how.

They began with Bologna (1088), followed by Oxford (1096), Paris (1200) and then a host of others, Naples by 1224. All of them, some 72 by the 15th Century, believe it or not, 'developed primarily out of the need of the reformed Church.'

Almost all university teachers were clerics and 'the most active agents in their spread were the reform popes who wished to see a rationally intelligible theology elaborated in response to controversies within the Church' *(Christian Social Witness, 142)*.

Greece, Rome, Byzantium, Islam and China did have higher education, but nothing like this medieval, now modern, institution. The university became a community of teachers with rights, possessing administrative autonomy, the power to determine curricula, the right of research, the ability to grant publicly recognised degrees *(Christian Social Witness, 141)*.

Prior to this turning point, education was provided by monasteries and cathedral schools, although they declined with the demise of the cities as feudalism arose.

The Third Lateran Council (1179) confirmed that education should be free. Benefices supported the masters and academics, which would later lead to elitism and careerism, but there can be no doubting this important historical moment.

Roman law was revived and the re-emergence of Greek thought through Islamic scholars needs to be appreciated. They re-introduced the thought of Aristotle, but their translations and commentaries needed purification.

William of Moerbeck (1215-86), a Flemish Dominican, provided more accurate translations from the Greek. It enabled St. Thomas Aquinas (1225-1274), not proficient in

Greek, to become prolific with a novel theological approach, combining faith and reason, enduring to this day. This was a truly remarkable development of the communion of faith and reason, to be ignored, however, in subsequent centuries due to prejudice.

It was about this time (1150), too, that Europe experienced something of an economic renaissance. Venice, with its sixty or so islands (inlets), obtained everything bar salt from trade. A commercial culture was created that was able to weather starvation, plagues, wars and economic depression with the merchant class aiding trade.

After the Avignon Papacy (1304-1376) was resolved, the renaissance, with its emphasis on classical literature, ancient languages, the individual, and the delights of civilised life, naturally emerged *(Christian Social Witness, 162)*.

Michelangelo was co-opted to re-build St. Peter's in Rome. Pope Julius II (1503-13) was a patron of the arts, but sale of indulgences to meet the cost of the building fueled Luther's revolt. It was not until Pope Paul III (1534-48) that reform came – but it was too late.

The protest against Rome would be deep and lasting. Christendom was finished. The Protestant Church would split into many denominations, not to be unified under Rome. The Christian Church was significantly weakened. The alignment of Church and State in the process of being annulled.

A counter reformation, launched by the Catholic Church, became more doctrinal, too defensive, less biblical, probably more pietistic, certainly more disciplined especially in its formation of priests. Charles notes:

> *The Catholic crowned heads of Europe were almost at one in seeking to limit as much as possible the influence of the reforming international Church, personified in the Papacy (Christian Social Witness, 2).*

Revolutions Writ Large

The modern world was emerging and it was through the 'gates' of Revolutions, the Enlightenment and the Industrial Revolution that it would do so, with the age of Kings coming to an end.

First the revolution in Britain (1642-49, 1688), then America (1776-81), then France (1789).

Civil war reigned in Britain from 1642-46 with the Parliament and King clashing. The King was defeated and Charles I executed in 1649. Charles II seemingly intended to restore Catholicism to England, but rebellion ensued, though not another civil war. The King hung on.

But his brother James II (1685-88) did not. He was usurped by his daughter Mary, married to William of Orange. It became known as the 'Glorious Revolution.'

Meanwhile, the Americans, seeking to remain under the

umbrella of the British, grew exasperated by George III's taxation plans to fund defence of the colonies. They were led by Samuel Adams of Boston.

By May 1776, the Virginia Convention was pushing independence. The *Declaration of Independence* – 4 July 1776 – clearly relied on the developing Western European tradition:

> *We hold these truths to be self-evident, that all men are created equal, that they are endowed by their Creator with certain inalienable rights, that among these are life, liberty and the pursuit of happiness.*

Charles astutely observes that the revolution succeeded by violence, but 'it went on to institute government under the law without any intervening period of chaos.'

Furthermore, the leaders of the revolution and the authors of the constitutions, both state and federal, were mainly university graduates. 'For them liberty was liberty under the law, and representative government was limited by the natural law as were all governments' *(Christian Social Witness, 279)*.

The aroma of the Magna Carta was definitely in the air. The universities were yielding results.

Charles' description of the French Revolution is nothing short of fascinating *(Christian Social Witness, 280-286)*. The *immediate* cause seems to have been the failure of Louis XVI's (1774-1792) fiscal reforms in 1789, arousing resentment among the three 'estates' (clergy, nobility, commoners) present in France at that time.

The *remote* causes of the revolution were undoubtedly repeated wars conducted by Louis XIV (1643-1715), rapacity in taxation methods, violence, and poverty through famines.

Sporadic rebellions and brutal retaliations were experienced in Boulonnais, Béarn, Bordeaux, Brittany and Paris between 1662 and 1709:

> *Twelve hundred men taken after the rising in Boulonnais were either broken on the wheel or hanged. The trees along the roads were strung with the bodies of the rebels captured after the defeat in Brittany (Christian Social Witness, 281).*

Famine was a constant. St. Vincent de Paul (1581-1660) was told of 'hordes of peasants,' 'searching like pigs for roots of the earth.' But then between 1740 and 1775 there was prosperity. By 1789 the population was 26 million, up from 18 million in 1715.

The harvest failed in 1788, the fiscal reforms of 1789 went down like a bomb, the 'bourgeois mob' stormed the Bastille (14 July 1789), a mass insurrection ensued in the countryside. The Revolution soon took 'an anti-clerical and anti-religious turn' and 'on 2 November it decreed that the Church should surrender her lands and the clergy would be paid by the state.'

Pope Pius VI opposed the Revolution, as did others, upon which the Papal States were seized and the pope imprisoned, dying in gaol in 1799, still reigning. His successor too was jailed, but lived to see the end of Napoleon in 1815.

All of this was the end of Church/State relations under monarchy. But as Charles comments, paradoxically the revolutionary forces, which swept away monarchies and thumped the Church, eventually liberated the Church to do what she does best – carry on missionary activity.

Enlightenment and the Industrial Revolution

The industrial revolution is widely understood to have begun in the middle of the 18th Century in Britain, subsequently spreading like a wave to other countries in Europe and the United States.

The world was being transformed from an agrarian economy – farming and handicraft – to an industrial one, with new forms of power and machinery. Britain gave birth to two important figures who championed the new scientific approach, which enabled the revolution – Francis Bacon (1561-1626) and Isaac Newton (1642-1727).

From Bacon we gained the inductive method of reasoning, with its emphasis on careful observation of nature and its events, 'leading to the establishment of the Royal Society in 1660' *(Land of Dreams, 45).*

Newton bequeathed to us his three laws, which as one fine engineer has cleverly observed, 'dictate how things move and explains why planes fly and, perhaps more importantly, why bridges stay still.' In addition, Newton's Law of Gravity has been a more than helpful insight in understanding the dynamics of the earth and beyond.

Can we see an underlying pattern with these movements, as the Middle Ages gives way to Renaissance, Reformation, Revolutions, the Enlightenment and industrial development?

Kemp seems to have captured the essence of the matter:

> *Implicit in the concepts of a more liberal politics and of a rational science was the idea that authority could be rightly questioned.*
>
> *The scientific approach encouraged technology, and its successes emboldened philosophers to extend this application of reason from the understanding of the natural and physical world to the understanding of human society itself.*
>
> *It was this effort to understand society 'scientifically,' pursued by European and British thinkers through the seventeenth and eighteenth centuries, that in turn led to the revolution in secular and moral thinking that is now generally referred to as the Enlightenment (Land of Dreams, 45).*

We judge previous generations with *hindsight* – something not at their disposal. But if those in authority, church and monarchy, had been more open to reason, then authority might have suffered fewer blows and maintained credibility.

Aquinas with his new dialogical approach in the 13th Century deeply respected both faith and reason. He was admired by a few, but suspected and censured. It was unfortunate. The evolution of society in subsequent centuries could have been made a little easier.

Still, looking back upon the journey humanity has made from the time of the Greeks, the Roman Empire, through the Christian world, until the advent of the Industrial Revolution, we sense something transcending human understanding, volition and toil.

History is our witness.

Despite the 'to-ing and fro-ing,' inevitable in human existence, at times quite brutal and violent, we seem to sense a providence, an 'invisible hand,' that both respects and directs the interplay of freedoms that history undoubtedly is.

Locating the beginnings of Australia within this wider context is more than helpful. Trying to understand the cultural, political and economic dynamics of a country without such a context would be unwise.

II

'What happened and Why'

The First Fleet set sail from England in May 1787 and arrived in Australia in January 1788. The first Governor was Arthur Phillip.

There were 11 ships, six carrying approximately 750 convicts – the majority found guilty of larceny, one woman for every seven men – the remainder being either civil or military personnel. Of the 1,420 persons who began the sea voyage, 1,373 made it.

America ceased the transportation of convicts to their country in the late 18th Century, having received perhaps 50,000. Australia was about to become 'the fatal shore.'

Surprisingly, sooner than expected, 'the struggle for survival was over.' In just 12 years, by 1800, the colony had 6,000 inhabitants, by 1822 it had 40,000. John McDonald *(Art of Australia: Exploration to Federation 2008, 57)* tells us of ex-convicts, emancipists, who created a rudimentary market for art:

> *The first subject turned to by artist and publisher, was the growth of the city itself ... the first 'views' were published by the emancipist brewer, Absalom West, in March 1812. The artist was another emancipist, John Eyre and the engraver, a convict named Philip Slaeger.*
>
> *It proved a successful venture, and West issued a further set of twelve views in January 1813. By September 1814, he was able to advertise a full set of 24 prints for the price of £9.*

'The fatal shore' was being transformed into a 'Garden of Eden,' denoting 'delight,' perhaps 'pleasure.'

What happened and why?

Early Explorers

The Dutch had discovered Australia in 1606, landing in Cape York. The Spanish, later that year, sailed through and navigated the Torres Strait Islands. In the 17th Century, some 29 Dutch explorers would navigate the western and southern coasts of *New Holland,* as they named it.

In June 1767, Captain Sam Wallis, in his English ship the *Dolphin,* discovered and explored a cluster of islands in the South Pacific, the 'most tantalising' being Tahiti:

> *Their leisurely way of life, and abundance of food and apparent abundance of sexual activity, excited the sailors from the Dolphin during their brief stay*

(Captain Cook's Epic Voyage 2020, 1).

Geoffrey Blainey, in his fascinating work on Cook's adventures, notes that from Greek and Roman times there was mistaken belief that a huge southern continent was located somewhere between New Holland and South America.

When the *Dolphin* returned home with news of the discovery of the islands, a French merchant ship set out, as did a British ship named the *Endeavour*, 'not much larger in area than a tennis court.'

The *Endeavour* carried scientists. The French ship carried silks. The scene was set, a pattern established, for the development of Australia with the mindset of modernity, not antiquity, doing its best to displace old world views and their consequences.

James Cook was born in 1728, just one year after the death of Newton. The scientific method was enhancing naval exploration, too. Cook's mother was English, his father Scottish, beginning the substantial influence of thought and personages from Scotland on Australia.

Cook's voyage, 'one of the most remarkable in recorded history,' uncovered no southern continent, but went on to navigate 'most of the coast of New Zealand' and 'to explore' for the first time, as far as we know, 'a vast stretch of the east coast of Australia' *(Captain Cook's Epic Voyage, ix)*.

Cook had a flair for mathematics not spelling, his journals

reveal, and loved astronomy, 'immersing himself' in Leadbetter's *A Compleat System of Astronomy.* He became the champion of computing longitude, 'the devil's own task' in the 1760's.

A transit of Venus across the face of the sun was expected on 3 June 1769. The next transit expected 105 years later. If the transit could be timed with great accuracy and observed from different points in the world, with the distance between the points known, then the distance between the sun and the earth could be calculated accurately, and that would be handy.

The newly founded *Royal Society* was key to this expedition to Tahiti, with King George III, a lover of science and technology, providing £4000. Cook was to lead the expedition to observe the transit, after which 'he was to open his secret instructions.'

Accompanying Cook on board the *Endeavour* were Joseph Banks and Daniel Solander, a botanist and a naturalist. It was a first for European exploration. The *Endeavour* was on an international quest for knowledge. It was to be 'mission accomplished.'

The transit having been observed, not with total satisfaction, Cook set sail for New Zealand, discovered by Abel Tasman at least a century earlier, then Australia.

On the 28 April 1770 the Endeavour entered Botany Bay, originally named Stingrays Harbour. Blainey says the 'unique plants on its shores supplanted the sea as the source of wonder' *(The Story of Australia's People: The Rise and Fall of Ancient Australia 2015, 246).*

Cook died on his third voyage in the Pacific in February 1779, clubbed and stabbed to death in Hawaii. Only two of his six children outlived him. His wife, Elizabeth, died in 1835, aged 93.

'The Fatal Shore'

In England, Banks began to advocate British settlement for Botany Bay in 1779. Convicts could be sent there, not cheaply, but it would help increase England's sea power in the region, enabling commercial advantage. The decision was made.

King George III interviewed Phillip in January 1787. He was commissioned with wide powers to control and defend the territory of New South Wales, as Cook had named it, with legislative and executive power.

He could 'establish courts, raise military forces, resist enemies, grant lands, fair marts and markets.' It would be executive rule, but by law, until free institutions could be established. It was clear what the attitude was to be with the native peoples:

> *You are to endeavour by every possible means to open an intercourse with the natives, and to conciliate their affection, enjoining all our subjects to live in amity and kindness with them (Land of*

Dreams, 67).

Perpetrators of violence were 'to be brought to punishment according to the degree of the offence.'

Blainey notes Phillip's sympathy for the Aborigines, not shared by convicts who escaped. 'On the edge of the settlement, Aborigines were shot and British marines and convicts were speared.' The attitude of those in authority was one thing, the actions of subjects another.

Phillip had particular clarity about one matter. It would be shared by successive governors:

> *There is one that I would wish to take place from the moment his Majesty's forces take possession of the country – there can be no slavery in a free land and consequently no slaves (Land of Dreams, 67).*

The first years were difficult. The colony could not produce enough food:

> *The soil was sandy and poor, the clearing of the tree stumps and roots was heavy work, and the tools and implements were meagre: the colony lacked even a plough until 1796 (The Story of Australia's People, 265).*

Phillip thought hanging was futile as a deterrent. He believed in humanitarian reform practices. But with the shortage of food and the theft that ensured, he thought the better of it. In 'March 1789 six guilty privates in His Majesty's Marines were led to the gallows' for robbery.

The other marines were assembled to witness the event.

Most convicts whose sentences had been completed remained in Australia, preferring to receive a grant of 12 hectares of land if single, or 40 hectares if married with five children. Food rations for a year were supplied, as were farming tools.

Phillip left in December 1792, accompanied by two Aborigines, four kangaroos, several dingoes, rare birds and plants and some ex-convicts. The 'mother country' must have been fascinated when he disembarked. A succession of governors was to follow.

'Garden of Eden'

From a population of just over 1,000 in 1788, the colony grew to 437,665 by 1851. Executive rule by governors would cease in 1854, giving way to self-government of sorts.

Governor Hunter followed Phillip in 1794, King arrived in 1800, Bligh in 1806, before he was 'sacked' by the mob in 1808. The first four governors were all of Royal Navy background.

Macquarie ruled for 12 years until 1822, Brisbane briefly governed until 1825, Darling until 1831. Bourke then arrived and persevered until 1838, while Gipps had eight years of governing until 1846, and Fitzroy was to be the last, finishing in 1854.

Kemp is complimentary, recommending them as 'men committed to the emerging schools of thought in Britain' at that time. He claims that they believed:

> *In a moral and civil public life, the separation of public and private interests, in humanitarian reform, in legal equality for all social classes and religions, in a high degree of social equality, and in the social and economic value of individual freedom (Land of Dreams, 48).*

'The emerging schools of thought' centred in and around the dignity and freedom of the human person, seeking 'to make it the organising principle for human society' *(Land of Dreams, 9).*

The Middle Ages had sown the seeds of modernity and the Revolutions had abruptly brought about change, dismantling the old order.

But what was left? What did the replacement look like?

Exactly how *would* a society be organised – politically, culturally, economically – honouring human reason, freedom and the rule of law? *Could* it actually be done?

It would have to be a partnership of thought and practice, an intimate one.

The governors were the men who 'pulled it off.' They knew the theory and were practical, each of them making significant contributions. Who were they?

Hunter, King, Macquarie

Hunter was a respected and competent officer in the Royal Navy, involved in campaigns against the French and Americans. He received a classical education and published a book on the colony, after captaining the *Sirius*, the supply ship of the First Fleet. 'He was a keen naturalist.'

King was commandant of Norfolk Island in 1788, returned home in 1790, but found himself boomeranged to Norfolk to sort out a 'mutinous element.' He became governor in September 1800:

> *He continued to seek good relations with the Aboriginal people, refused to allow them to be worked as slaves, and said he 'ever considered them the real proprietors of the soil.'*
>
> *He also emphasised reform of the convicts, and employed a number of convicts who had served their terms (emancipists) in his administration (as had Hunter) (Land of Dreams, 80).*

King confronted the trading monopoly of the military, increasing supply from imports and government farms. Whaling and sealing were encouraged. He established settlements in Van Dieman's Land.

Quickly, the colony was assuming great flexibility, providing incentives to convicts to reform, unique in the Empire at that time. They were permitted to hold property, despite English law to the contrary. They could be 'administrators, architects, accountants, painters and artists.'

Because of the productivity of the colony's economy, King was able to reduce government rations from 72 per cent of the population in 1800 to 32 per cent in 1806. Remarkable.

He imposed a 5 per cent duty on imports of non-British goods, establishing a school for orphan girls from the revenues. Several day schools were government supervised *(Land of Dreams, 81)*. A free and fair country was in embryo.

King's conflict with the New South Wales Corps exhausted him. He died back home in 1808. William Bligh, too, was from the Royal Navy:

> *A man of considerable attainments, personal courage, a skilled maker of charts, a close associate of Sir Joseph Banks, a gold-medal winner from the Royal Society of Arts for his reports on his South Sea explorations and a fellow of the Royal Society for 'distinguished services in navigation, botany' (Land of Dreams, 82).*

But Bligh had his weaknesses. He was authoritarian, 'difficult to get on with, and given to flights of foul language.'

It was a barter economy, spirits the favoured product of trade. Bligh tackled it head on. This, and his questioning of leases held by some officers, including John Macarthur, finished him up. On 26 January 1808, Bligh was taken into custody by a coup. Courage there was, but recklessness too.

Governor Lachlan Macquarie arrived in 1810. Like Cook, he was a Scot, but from the army, not the navy. As were the earlier governors, he was of deeply humane instincts' *(Land of Dreams, 84).*

Wilberforce encouraged Macquarie to pay attention to the religious and moral culture of the colony, as did Lord Castlereagh, Secretary of State for the Colonies:

> *The Great Objects of Attention are to improve the Morals of the Colonists, to encourage Marriage, to provide for Education, to prohibit the use of Spirituous Liquors, to increase the Agriculture and Stock, so as to ensure the Certainty of a full supply to the Inhabitants under all Circumstances (Land of Dreams, 84).*

Macquarie was a benevolent autocrat, governing without an executive council, with a typical Scottish egalitarian outlook. Upon arrival in the colony he was intrigued and delighted no doubt to find a 'society in which many skilled and even professional tasks were being performed by convicts and former convicts' *(Land of Dreams, 85).*

By 1814 a civil court was established, not hearing criminal matters as there was as yet no trial by jury. The development of infrastructure during his governorship was impressive, as was his treatment of convicts:

> *Once a convict has become a free man he should in all respects be considered on a footing with every other man in the colony, according to his rank in life*

or character (Land of Dreams, 88).

William Charles Wentworth (1790-1872) was the first Australian-born political leader, instrumental in obtaining constitutional self-government. He was educated in England, returning in 1811, appointed by Macquarie as acting provost marshal and being granted 1,750 acres on the Nepean River. He crossed the Blue Mountains with Blaxland and Lawson in 1813.

He was opposed to the 'colonial aristocracy' – free settlers who thought they were the upper class. Wentworth wanted a society based on merit. While admiring Macquarie as a man, he disliked the emphasis placed on public works to the detriment of establishing the conditions necessary for the functioning of enterprise in the colony.

Because of Wentworth's influence limited constitutional government, via an appointed *Legislative Council*, was established with the New South Wales Act 1823. Importantly, a Supreme Court was established, so also, trial by jury in civil cases, 'a crucial step in the establishment of the rule of law in Australia.'

Francis Forbes, another Scot, was the Chief Justice of the Supreme Court, labelled by the *Sydney Herald* (1837) as 'the great leader of 'Liberalism' *(Land of Dreams, 102).*

Macquarie left in 1822, with Brisbane, yet another Scot, the next governor. Wentworth's influence again was tangible, for his policy brief focused not on public works, but on public and private economy, and further constitutional development.

Brisbane and Darling

Brisbane, too, was an 'enlightened' man, with a strong interest in astronomy, elected as a Fellow of the *Royal Society* in 1810. In him NSW received a civilised, well-educated and connected governor.

Besides trying to phase out transportation and increase free settlers, Brisbane was just in his treatment of all citizens, particularly emancipists, religious groups and supported an Aboriginal reserve.

Wentworth had returned from Britain in 1824 with a printing press with Englishman Robert Wardell, later to be murdered. Together they established *The Australian* newspaper, highly critical of future Governor Darling. The opening editorial penned by Wardell highlights the desire and the struggle to establish a free and fair country:

> *A free press is the most legitimate, and, at the same time, the most powerful weapon that can be employed to annihilate influence, frustrate the designs of tyranny, and restrain the arm of oppression (Land of Dreams, 103).*

Darling replaced Brisbane in 1825, the year Van Dieman's land became a separate colony. He was not sympathetic to liberalism, but it was a time of continued 'transformation of the colonial government' 'and the further strengthening of the legal and monetary framework for the market and private enterprise economy' *(Land of Dreams, 105).*

Bourke and Gipps

Richard Bourke replaced Darling in 1831. The reform movement was in full swing. Bourke enabled it handsomely:

> *For the first time a self-consciously liberal regime set out to promote the rule of law, a liberal economy, social equality, reform of the convict system, freedom of the press, freedom of religion, universal education, protection of native peoples and a moral law-abiding culture (Land of Dreams, 117).*

Bourke was Irish, a distant relative of Edmund Burke, charming, loved by friends and family.

A 'bounty' scheme of immigration began in 1835, aiming to attract skilled migrants. It succeeded spectacularly. In 1828 there were 36,000 in the colony. By 1841 the number was 119,000. The culture, ideas and skills of the colony were enhanced. Land grants were abolished in 1831, replaced by sale, yet the influx of settlers meant temporary loss of control in the inland plains.

Bourke's liberal credentials and achievements were ubiquitous. In 1831 he proposed and received Colonial Office approval for non-military juries in criminal cases, with emancipists sitting on juries. He 'believed the colony was ready for an elected legislature' *(Land of Dreams, 156)*. His Church Act of 1836 provided support to all denominations, but he ran into opposition in trying to establish a system of public education. Sectarianism provided the blockage.

What Went Right? What Went Wrong?

Charles Darwin arrived in Sydney Cove in 1836, the year 'the Benthamite colony of South Australia was becoming established.' He was a witness to the flourishing colony:

Here, in a less promising country, scores of years have done many times more than an equal number of centuries have effected in South America.

The streets are regular, broad, clean and kept in excellent order; the houses are of good size, and the shops well furnished ... not even near London or Birmingham is there an appearance of such rapid growth (Land of Dreams, 166).

A statue of Governor Bourke was erected in 1842, just four years after he retired. Funded by public contributions, it is found in Macquarie Street, Sydney.

The extraordinary inscription that accompanies the statue recognises 'his able, honest and benevolent administration.'

Listing the many achievements during his tenure – amelioration of penal discipline, publication of public receipts and expenditure, immigration, religious equality, foundation of Port Phillip, establishment of savings banks, a tribunal for land grants and claims, liberty of press, extension of trial by jury – it finishes with a flourish:

He raised the colony to unexampled prosperity, and retired amid the reverent and affectionate regret of the people, having won their confidence by his integrity, their gratitude by his services, their admiration by his public talents, and their esteem by his private worth (Land of Dreams, 186).

Former private secretary to Lord Auckland, first Lord of the Admiralty, George Gipps became governor in 1838, at a time of severe drought, leading to depression. Gipps thought that speculation and private extravagance funded by debt did not help. Wisely, he refused to provide assistance to those on the path to bankruptcy.

Gipps would have eight years in authority. The depression was enduring, but he sustained immigration and the population doubled to over 190,000. He had to face the 'unstoppable occupation without title of the inland plains' *(Land of Dreams, 211).*

The original approach of restraining settlement could not possibly work, given the sheer size of the country and its increasing inhabitants. He had to settle with opening the lands to the 'many,' thereby impeding ownership by the 'few,' with sensible regulations.

The issue highlighted a fundamental social and political principle of the colony – *self-interest gives way to public-interest.*

Gipps, in accord with Colonial Office policy, prepared the way for self-government with elections of sorts held in 1843.

He was 'humane, practical and courageous' with Aborigines. An 'Aboriginal Protectorate' was established in four provinces at Port Phillip in 1838, but Gipps noted that outrages against Aborigines 'are now of frequent occurrence beyond the boundaries of location.'

Twenty-eight indigenous men, women and children were slaughtered at Myall Creek in 1838. After the 11 accused were acquitted, Gipps insisted on a re-trial. Seven were found guilty and hanged.

On 10 June 2000 a memorial was erected at the site, with a yearly memorial celebration set in motion. The plaque at the Myall Massacre and Memorial Site reads:

> *In memory of the Wirrayaraay people who were murdered on the slopes of this ridge in an unprovoked but premeditated act in the late afternoon of 10 June 1838.*
>
> *Erected on 10 June 2000 by a group of Aboriginal and non-Aboriginal Australians in an act of reconciliation, and in acknowledgment of the truth of our shared history.*
>
> *We Remember them (Ngiyani winangay ganunga).*

Fitzroy arrived a month after the departure of Gipps, who left in poor health in July 1846. He died in February 1847. Kemp comments:

> *Under Richard Bourke and George Gipps the British colonies in eastern Australia had experienced fifteen years of principled liberal, although not democratic government (Land of Dreams, 239).*

Fitzroy was 'a sociable and friendly aristocrat, accustomed to deference,' 'shrewd, earthy judgement of men and events, robust health, and an obvious preference for peace at a not-too-unreasonable price.'

'A Principle is a Wedge'

Transportation to New South Wales had been discontinued in 1840, but not so Tasmania. It reared its ugly head again but with supposed reforms. Surprisingly, perhaps, Wentworth approved. Enter Henry Parkes (1815-1896), 'father' of Australian Federation and Charles Cowper (1807-1875), president of the Anti-Transportation League, five times Premier of New South Wales.

With plans afoot to separate Port Phillip in 1847 from New South Wales – Victoria becoming a colony in 1851 – transportation was to become 'Australia's first truly national issue.' It was to feed and arouse the desire for genuine self-government.

Two figures in Tasmania drove the Anti-Transportation campaign, native-born Richard Dry and Reverend John West; the latter conceiving the strategy. It was John West, who designed a flag for the campaign: the Southern Cross, on a blue background, Union Jack in the corner.

The blue represents 'justice,' the white banner 'purity,' the Union Jack representing 'no banner of rebellion,' the Cross symbolising 'looking forward to success, enabled by looking upward for support.' How many Australians understand the symbolism today?

West's insistence on *argument,* not *violence,* proved crucial for the culture of the colony:

> *We have, then, a mighty empire to contend against – one which can laugh our threatening to scorn. And what are the weapons we must employ? What but the weapons of truth (Land of Dreams, 332).*

He was good and clever.

'The colonists would say to Britain: Until you can with safety discharge the criminal into your community, he shall not enter ours.' 'We now have a new principle: and a principle is a wedge.' 'A community should deal with its own crime.'

The New South Wales Legislative Council met on 27 September 1850. 36,000 petitions against transportation were presented, 525 in favour. It was overwhelming.

Wentworth offered a well-researched defence, but to no avail. Debate ended on 1 October 1850. The will of the majority was conveyed by Fitzroy to Her Majesty. The same day saw the establishment of Australia's first university, the *University of Sydney*, founded by William Charles Wentworth.

The *Australasian League* (March 1851) was formed to ensure eradication of transportation to Tasmania. By the opening of the British parliament in late 1852 it was over, well and truly, with the Queen's Speech notifying.

Western Australia, originally named the *Swan River Colony*

(1829) persevered with convicts until 1868, receiving 9,000 from inception. All in all, 157,000 convicts were transported to Australia.

The age of the governors was coming to an end.

Representative Government

The fight to eliminate transportation went hand in hand with the struggle to have one's own constitution. The British Government invited the *Legislative Council* to draft up a constitution for the colony. Wentworth seized his opportunity.

He met opposition from the somewhat anarchical Parkes, not the idea itself, of course, but the type and character of the constitution.

Wentworth believed that representation should not be based on population, but on the 'great interests of the country.' He set sail on 20 March 1854 with royal assent given 16 July 1855. Elections were held in March and April 1856. The colony was to have four premiers by the end of 1857. The 'revolving door' hasn't stopped since.

The Victorians had a draft constitution up and running by 1854. Kemp argues forcibly that the cause for democracy was given impetus by the Gold Rush of the 1850's. Charles La Trobe was the Superintendent of Port Phillip from late 1839, and then appointed Lieutenant Governor in 1851.

The first governor of the colony of Victoria was Charles

Hotham (June 1854). He didn't last long. On his arrival he found around 80,000 miners from England, Scotland, Ireland, the United States, Germany, France, Italy and Sweden. There were also more than 10,000 Chinese present, mostly from southern China.

The truth and persuasiveness of Kemp's claim is manifest. Energetic and entrepreneurial men and women, endowed with the spirit of liberalism and democracy, arrived from around the globe. Their experience fueled the democratic and liberal spirit.

Hotham was unwise. Police were ordered to check mining licenses twice a week to help aid collection of revenue. History recounts the grave mistake, with 22 miners and six police soldiers killed on 3 December 1854. What became known as the *Eureka Stockade* acted as catalyst for change.

Elections, along the lines of New South Wales, were held in 1856. The parliament contained graduates from Oxford, Cambridge and Trinity College, Dublin. There were 60 members, four were native-born. Kemp lists the fascinating make-up:

> *In the new Assembly, the Scottish and the Irish equaled in number those from England (twenty-eight each). A majority were Anglican. There were seven Presbyterians, six Catholics and two Methodists, alongside ten independents.*
>
> *A third were merchants or traders, a fifth were pastoralists, ten were lawyers and there was one manufacturer (an iron-founder) (Land of Dreams, 414).*

Land of Dreams

A *Land Convention* met for the first time in July 1857. It was elected by the people to decide on, and demand, its own land policy. People wanted to realise their dreams in the *Land of Dreams*.

It was as effective as previous campaigns for land justice. Kemp summarises the magnificent achievement:

> *In 1860 and the years following, Land Acts were passed in Victoria and New South Wales to expand the opportunities for those with little or no capital to settle themselves on the land that had been occupied by the pastoralists (Land of Dreams, 442).*

The sheer size of the country and the paucity of 'instruments at their disposal' made administration of land quite difficult and complex, but nevertheless much was achieved:

> *Despite the legal difficulties, however, and the breakdown in many instances of law enforcement, the dream of the liberal reformers, and of the democrats who came after, that the land should be the possession of the many rather than the few was to be realised (Land of Dreams, 442).*

Undoubtedly, the development of railways through the 1860s to the 1880s enabled the huge continent to be opened up for settlement, facilitating transportation of products to cities and ports.

The just distribution of land and property is a perennial

issue for any nation. It is a struggle that each generation must face and engage in. Henry Parkes, at the *Australasian Federation Conference (1890),* noted the achievement in such a short space of time:

> *In reality, we stand at the head of the nations of the world in the distribution of wealth ... The real standard in civilisation is the wide diffusion of wealth over the population to be governed (David Kemp, A Free Country, 2-3).*

Although Australia has a proper and excellent legal framework, we now face a particular challenge. Despite our enormous land mass and small population, all of our major cities register in the worst 30 cities of the world when comparing the average annual wage to median house price.

This has not been the case for the majority of our history, especially so in the middle to later part of the 20th Century, when home ownership soared, aided by affordability.

As Australia continues her journey into the 21st Century we must recognise the potential for social disharmony that this challenge poses.

What is the recipe that will ensure continued access to land and property, a sure staple of social stability in a free and fair country?

Dreams are preferable to nightmares.

III

What went right?
What went wrong?

Australia became a federated nation on 1 January 1901.

The 1901 census counted 3,773,801 people. The median age was 22, thirty-five percent of the population under 15, four percent over 65.

The population had flourished. So, too, systems of education, means of communication, wealth creation and distribution. Wealth per head of the population outstripped every nation:

> *Wealth per head of the Australians was already the highest in the world: 'In Austria, it amounts to £16 6s; in Germany, to £18 14s; in France, to £25 14s; in the United Kingdom, to £35 4s; in the United States, to £39, and in Australasia, to £48.'*

Parkes claimed in 1891 that wealth distribution was unequalled by any other nation:

> *[J]udged by that test, Australasia stands at the head*

> *of the nations of the world, not only so, but a long way at the head (Kemp, A Free Country, 480).*

The Australian Constitution

A Constitutional Convention was held in 1891 and again in 1897-98, with royal assent given to the Constitutional Bill on 9 July 1900. The colonies were to become the States of Australia. It was time well spent.

Henry Parkes, an 'English-born poet, shopkeeper, newspaper editor-writer, and politician' came to Australia in 1839. He was five times premier of the colony of New South Wales, eventually receiving the title *'Father of Federation.'*

Parkes demonstrated his poetic ability at the beginning of the 1891 convention, highlighting the geographical and political uniqueness of Australia:

> *Our country is fashioned by nature in a remarkable manner – in a manner which distinguishes it from all other countries ... we ... are separated from all countries by a wide expanse of sea, which leaves us an immense territory ... capable of sustaining its countless millions – leaves us compact within ourselves, so that if a perfectly free people can arise anywhere, it surely may arise in this favoured land of Australia (Kemp, A Free Country, 479).*

Australian born Alfred Deakin (1856-1919), Prime

Minister of Australia three times (1903-04, 1905-08, 1909-10), said that Parkes had flaws but was nevertheless 'a large-brained, self-educated Titan, whose natural field was found in Parliament.'

Parkes loved the jousting of politics and parliament, but he also excelled in another 'natural field.' His first marriage to Clarinda Varney in 1836 yielded 12 children. Upon her death, he married Eleanor Dixon in 1889, having five children, three born before the marriage.

His second wife died in 1895. Parkes married a third time – Julia Lynch, his former cook and housekeeper. She was 23. Parkes by then was 80 years of age. He was to die a year later, with the federation well and truly in the pipeline.

Did the founders of the *Constitution of the Commonwealth of Australia* have their eyes on the Australian Flag, designed by Reverend John West for the *Anti-Transportation League* in the middle of the 19th Century. Recall the meaning of the flag:

> *The blue represents 'justice,' the white banner 'purity,' the Union Jack representing 'no banner of rebellion,' the Cross symbolising 'looking forward to success, enabled by looking upward for support.'*

The 'end' was a free and fair society. The 'means' were *not* to be rebellion and revolution. The *Southern Cross* was the symbol of temporal success, of justice, of reliance on the providence of God.

The *Federal Commonwealth of Australia* was understood

to be the work of human hands and the invisible hand of God. The preamble of the Constitution reads:

> *WHEREAS the people of New South Wales, Victoria, South Australia, Queensland, and Tasmania, humbly relying on the blessing of Almighty God, have agreed to unite in one indissoluble Federal Commonwealth under the Crown of the United Kingdom of Great Britain and Ireland, and under the Constitution hereby established.*

At the second Constitutional Convention in 1898, Deakin carried forth the poetic fervor of Parkes:

> *What a charter of liberty is embraced within this Bill – of political and religious liberty – the liberty and the means to achieve all to which men in these days can reasonably aspire.*
>
> *A charter of liberty is enshrined in this Constitution, which is also a charter of peace – peace, order and good government for the whole of the peoples whom it will embrace and unite (Kemp, A Free Country, 477).*

It is section 116 of the *Constitution of the Commonwealth of Australia* that protects religious liberty.

Why is it there?

It was placed in the 1898 Bill because the delegates at the Convention had been convinced by South Australian delegate Patrick McMahon Glynn (1855-1931) to insert 'reliance on God' in the preamble.

Deakin believed Glynn to be 'if not the best-read man of the Convention,' then certainly the man who 'carried more English prose and poetry in his memory than any three or four of his associates.'

Section 116 reads:

> *The Commonwealth shall not make any law for establishing any religion, or for imposing any religious observance, or for prohibiting the free exercise of any religion, and no religious test shall be required as a qualification for any office or public trust under the Commonwealth.*

No official religion. No compulsion in religion. No restriction on religion. No religious discrimination.

It could not be better put.

Many of the founders of course were *not* religious. Some had vague attachments to organised religion, a few were religious – mostly Christian, perhaps some Deists

With this knowledge, one begins to sense the importance of the provision. In fact, it protects a fundamental human right that when denied leads to chaos.

We are aware that the most fundamental human right is the *right to life*. Then follows the right to pursue and discover *the meaning of life*. This is what religious liberty means and proclaims.

These two rights – the right to life and its meaning – are intimately entwined.

To proclaim religious liberty, as the constitution does, is to proclaim this fundamental right, a right belonging to unbelievers and believers alike. The founders knew exactly what they were doing. The wisdom of the provision is displayed without ambiguity.

Every Australian has the right to search for the meaning of life. When satisfied with their seeking, they have the right to a *way of life* that accords with their beliefs, normally attempted and expressed in and through *communities.*

Naturally enough this right is forfeited when violence is employed. It is after all, a 'charter of liberty, a charter of peace.'

Edmund Barton, Australia's first Prime Minister (1901-1903) and then Justice of the High Court (1903-1920), believed the 1898 Bill was 'a more liberal constitution than the work of 1891.' He posed the questions and answered them:

> *Is this a Constitution which will enable a free people to come together, and in community together to work out their own destiny? Who can deny it?*
>
> *Is it a Constitution which gives all reasonable and liberal guarantees of freedom? That can only be answered in one way (Kemp, A Free Country, 507).*

The *American Commonwealth*, a classic three-volume

study of American politics and political science in general, was authored by James Bryce, yet another Scotsman. He thought that the Australian constitution:

> *Represents the high-water mark of popular government. It is penetrated by the spirit of democracy.*
>
> *The actual every day working of government in the Australian colonies is more democratic than in Britain, because Britain has retained certain oligarchical habits, political as well as social.*
>
> *It is more democratic than in the United States, because there both the States and the Union are fettered by many constitutional restrictions.*

Of real importance, with an insight that is more akin to hindsight, Bryce observed the intimate relationship between legislature and executive in the Australian Constitution:

> *In Australia the people, through their legislature with its short term, are not only supreme, but can, by their legislature's control of the Executive, give effect to their wishes with incomparable promptitude.*
>
> *For this purpose, the expression 'people' practically means the leader who for the time being commands the popular majority (Kemp, A Free Country, 514).*

What went right? The *Commonwealth of Australia Constitution Act*. Its defence of freedom and religious liberty, has been undervalued in Australia. Will it take on greater meaning and force in the 21st Century?

Misunderstandings about the nature of human freedom suggest so. *Self-interest* groups proclaim their rights, but fail to acknowledge the rights of others, thereby damaging *public interest*. Revisiting the notion of the *common good* will be essential.

White Australia Policy

Wealth and its distribution, land ownership, education, communication, freedom of religion, democratic institutions, a free press, and significant infrastructure were achieved by Federation.

Was Henry Parkes too utopian in his assessment of the colonies by the late 19th Century? What went wrong?

The events leading up to the Federation of Australia were challenging. Each of the colonies had rightly developed their own identities. At times it appeared that differences and difficulties might be insurmountable, rendering unity near impossible.

Of great significance was the intense debate and struggle between protectionism and free trade among the colonies. The Victorians had opted for tariffs, the New South Welshmen for free trade. The debates were fierce, but Federation was able to resolve the issue.

Whilst free trade within the States was assured by the Constitution, protectionism took the upper hand in international trade. And so too a restrictive immigration policy. Kemp calls it *'Walls against the world' (Kemp, A Democratic Nation, Chapter 2)*. He provides helpful context and assessment:

> *The decision to lead off the legislative program of the first parliament with a bill to restrict coloured immigration was seen by its proponents as politically sound ... It was justified by its proponents as a measure to remove the threat of racial conflict from the new nation and as a foundation for social harmony.*
>
> *It was nevertheless a policy choice whereby Australia rejected the ideal of multiracialism that liberalism and humanitarianism implied ... It was a policy choice that fed on prejudice rather than leading a fight against it (Kemp, A Democratic Nation, 45).*

The *Immigration of Restriction Act 1901* was drafted by Alfred Deakin and passed by the Barton Government. The *White Australia Policy* was put in place and persisted through the *Second World War.*

John Curtin, Australia's fourteenth Prime Minister, let it be known that Australia 'shall remain forever the home of the descendants of those people who came here in peace in order to establish in the South Seas an outpost of the British race.' Curtin, a great wartime leader, prophesied inaccurately. The *White Australia Policy* would slowly, but surely, be dismantled between the years 1949 and 1973.

Justified as 'removing the threat of racial conflict, but nevertheless 'failing to lead the fight against prejudice,' the *White Australia Policy* undoubtedly had its historical forerunners in the colonies.

The Colony of Queensland was keen on sugar-cropping, but inducing European labour to the tropics would require high wage rates. 'A traffic in low-wage islander labour' was commenced.

Kemp reports that 'it was estimated that some 46,000 islanders were brought to Australia, and their mortality rate far exceeded that of European labour' *(Kemp, A Free Country, 189)*. The figure represented approximately one-third of the number of convicts transported from Britain.

Samuel Griffith (1845-1920), Premier of Queensland (1883-88, 1890-1893) was not impressed:

> *The trade at its inception having been 'as bad as the African slave trade, at its very worst.' He said 'that every man was procured by force or fraud' and that 'if the sugar industry could not be supported without recourse to such means, it was better that it should go' (Kemp, A Free Country, 189).*

Was he prophesying and articulating the arguments for a *Just Wage*, established in Australia in the early 20th Century? Legislation attempted to end the trade after 31 December 1890, with commonsense eventually prevailing. Desires to have North Queensland declared a separate state dissipated.

The discovery of gold in the middle of the 19th Century resulted in labour shortages. Over 3,000 Chinese labourers came to the colony of New South Wales between 1848 and 1852. They came from Hong Kong, a newly established British colony. The Victorian goldfields accommodated some 42,000 Chinese by 1859. In Queensland (1875-77) there were 17,000 Chinese mining for gold, compared to just 2,000 Europeans.

The gold ran out in the southern colonies. Many Chinese returned home, but some moved north to New South Wales. By 1861 there were still 38,742 Chinese in Australia, 21,000 in New South Wales.

A liberal society is presumably 'colour-blind.' Yet why is it that Parkes passed a *Chinese Restriction Act* in 1888? Kemp gives a number of probable reasons.

Australia was a British settlement and should remain so. Many of the Chinese immigrants seemed to be under the control of people in China. Their commitment to Australia was questioned. The argument was nationalistic and culturally based.

The Chinese were willing to work for lower wages. Parkes had used his newspaper, the *Empire,* to campaign against the importation of Chinese slaves and condemned pastoralists seeking cheap labour. The Chinese 'were carriers of vice, especially of drugs such as opium' *(Kemp, A Free Country, 469-471)*. Moral reasons were offered for restriction.

Racial arguments abounded. The Chinese were regarded as

'biologically inferior.' Deakin, in fact, argued at the 1891 Convention that the issue of Asian immigration would be best dealt with by a national government:

> *A united Australia will be called upon to face the largest problems. One has been in some measure already dealt with, but not yet finally solved – the influx of inferior races into the northern parts of the continent.*

The Chinese were to be excluded in the latter part of the 19th Century. It is said that on the goldfields the Chinese, to a large extent, 'stuck together.' Why wouldn't they? Their language was different, their culture foreign to the colonies. The next generation would have found integration easier.

Was there another 'piece to the puzzle' giving insight why a nation, seeking a free and fair country, would, at its federal inception, establish a *White Australia Policy*, not even allowing restricted access to coloured people, especially of Asian background?

Whilst Cook and the governors had appreciated and proclaimed the goodness of Australia's indigenous peoples, they nevertheless could not control the violence unleashed upon those who inhabited Australia approximately 65,000 years ago.

Our First Nation's Peoples

The First Fleet had brought 1,373 people in 1788. The indigenous population at that time 'uncertainly estimated' to be 300,000, perhaps even 750,000 persons:

> *It has been estimated that by 1901 those of Aboriginal descent numbered only some 110,000, including many now – as a result of relations with settlers – with European ancestry.*
>
> *Decline was the consequence of disease, violence (including poison), destruction of hunting grounds and demoralisation (Kemp, A Free Country, 172).*

The reversal of 'populations' was as dramatic as it was symbolic. It was C.S. Lewis who said,

> *God whispers to us in our pleasures, speaks in our conscience, shouts in our pains.*

Consciences have now been aroused to face the 'darkness, emptiness and chaos' that is undeniably part of our history. Whispers have become candid speech and shouts of pain are no longer ignored.

Kemp relies on the latest research. Australian historian Lyndall Ryan, author of *Tasmanian Aborigines: A History Since 1803 (2012)*, editor of *Theatres of Violence: Massacre, Mass Killing and Atrocity throughout History (2012)*, has recently produced *Colonial Frontier Massacres in Eastern Australia 1788-1930*, an online resource containing the 'Map.'

One of the aims of this historical work is to 'provide the first Australia wide record of frontier massacres that is comprehensive, based on a rigorous methodology, with well-structured data and a map, and providing the available evidence for each frontier massacre site.'

Combined with Kemp's presentation of statistics, Ryan's work leaves us with an undeniable and clear picture of what happened as colonists moved to the frontiers. Kemp began his five volume work with these words:

> *Dreaming and Australia have been linked from time immemorial. The culture of the Aboriginal people who first settled the land and nurtured it for perhaps 60,000 years centred on the Dreaming (Kemp, Land of Dreams, 3).*

Trauma consciousness is now recognised, fuelled no doubt by the experience of world wars and their effects. A work in progress, it is now acknowledged as a serious 'wound,' calling forth social, psychological, psychiatric and spiritual help.

Is it possible that a culture, so given over to story-telling and 'dreaming,' has not retained the horrific memories of these massacres? And is the consequence of that the 'intergenerational trauma,' which is so viscerally displayed in many, it not all, present day indigenous communities?

Facing the truth is like facing the light. Initially we are blinded by it, but slowly but surely the light begins to enlighten, penetrate and liberate – as it has done and will continue to do.

The First Hundred Years

The colony of South Australia gave women the right to vote and allowed them to stand for parliament in 1894. It was a world's first, an important foundational liberal reform. The Australian Federation achieved political equality for men and women in 1902 – just behind New Zealand.

John Stuart Mill (1806-1873), of Scottish heritage, was a leading British philosopher and liberal thinker, including equal rights for women. He published deeply influential works – *Principles of Political Economy* (1848) and *On Liberty* (1859). Karl Marx (1818-1883) was a German philosopher, and in collaboration with Friedrich Engels (1820-1895), published *The Communist Manifesto* (1847). It too was persuasive.

Both men had reform agendas. Were they seeking a similar society – a classless, humane, more equal one? Perhaps, but the 'means' were radically different.

Marx and Engels believed a classless society could be wrought through abolition of private property, inevitable class struggle and revolution of the working classes (proletariat) over capitalists (bourgeoisie), and centralisation of the means of communication and transport by the state.

Mill, for his part, believed deeply in individual liberty and in a just distribution of wealth. He was opposed to *laissez-faire* economics because such a society subordinated humane values to production. Rather, he focused on production, distribution and exchange in free economies. He followed Adam Smith's deeply human instincts, recognising the 'sympathy,' not 'antagonism,' that exists between people, giving rise to mutual exchanges that benefit both parties. The approach was deeply at odds with the *Manifesto*.

Mill was critical of property laws favouring the 'few at the expense of the many,' whereby a system of inheritance conferred property on those who never worked for it. Of utmost importance, for the development of a free and fair society, Mill expounded the principle of private property:

> *Private property, in every defence of it, is supposed to mean the guarantee to individuals of the fruits of their own labour and abstinence.*
>
> *The guarantee to them of the fruits of the labour and abstinence of others, transmitted to them without any merit or exertion of their own, is not of the essence of the institution (Kemp, Land of Dreams, 293 – citing Mill 1848).*

Mill's argument is compelling. Private property is the great 'guarantee' of the exertion and thriftiness of citizens. A just *legal framework* for private property therefore is essential to liberal reform and represents the most 'natural mechanism' available that a society has for the just distribution of wealth.

Both Mill and Marx would have their adherents in the Australian colonies in the 19th Century and the Federation itself. During the 20th Century the struggle between these two competing reform agendas would ebb and flow, present in various ways in political and civil life. Kemp provides us with a fascinating narrative in volumes three *(A Democratic Nation)* and four *(A Liberal State)* of his work.

Social philosophies associated with Marxism (Communism), such as Socialism, were attractive and continue to be so to some groups within Australian society, sometimes associated with more radical elements of the Australian Labor Party (1891) and the Labour Movement, but not exclusively so.

This is especially true during times of war and depression, which accounts for the first half of the 20th Century. Times of crisis fuel the instinct to 'gather and collect' the resources of a nation in defence of its subjects. But even in peacetime and more tranquil periods there will always be debates about how much and what type of state intervention is required to ensure freedom and fairness.

The Communist Party was founded in 1920, gathering perhaps 20,000 members by the mid-1940s. It was banned by the Liberal Government in 1950, but the High Court overturned the legislation in 1951.

Liberty was the victor and she was for the bulk of the 20th Century, despite constant and powerful setbacks.

The two World Wars left deep wounds. Just under 417,000 men enlisted for *World War I*, taken from a population of nearly five million. It was an extraordinary contribution.

Over 62,000 men and women lost their lives – with approximately 200,000 seriously injured. Joan Beaumont calls it a *Broken Nation (2014)*.

World War II exacted its price too. Between the two world wars a pandemic raged and economic disaster hit. Beaumont to the rescue again with her insightful analysis – *Australia's Great Depression: How a nation shattered by the Great War survived the worst economic crisis it has ever faced (2022)*.

She argues 'the democratic system generally proved robust,' the labour movement didn't go feral since it was represented by the Australian Labor Party whose 'ideological commitment to socialism was ambiguous,' – 'fearing communism as much as did the conservatives.'

Australian governments, including local councils, were able to create 'systems of sustenance and relief works.' Intermediary institutions, 'charities, churches, schools, professional organisations, trade union collectives and returned soldier's organisations' provided 'powerful philanthropic impulse.'

Beaumont argues that the most 'natural' of societies rose to the challenge:

> *No form of community was as important to societal resilience as the family. Be it nuclear or extended, a functioning family provided practical support and emotional security at a time of extraordinary dislocation and acute anxiety.*

She lets personal resilience have the 'last word,' providing a more than adequate 'road map' for our future:

> *It is clear that many individuals were able in times of profound crisis and hardship to draw on a mix of personal attributes, temperament and environment to ward off the worst effects of trauma.*
>
> *In retrospect this generation of Australians inspires a certain awe. Many of them had lived through World War I, losing sons, fathers and husbands to the great industrialised warfare. Many carried terrible physical and mental injuries from that conflict and the cruel pandemic that followed it. Many fell back on the assurances of the still dominant Christian faith that the struggles of this world were an intrinsic part of the human condition, leading to rewards in the life to come (Beaumont, Australia's Great Depression, 453-60).*

Robert Menzies gave liberty a new voice. The Prime Minister, who read poetry before giving speeches, echoed, after the trauma of the first 50 years after Federation, the importance of respecting the dignity and freedom of the human person.

Menzies embarked on a series of weekly radio broadcasts from January 1942 to April 1944, totalling 105. The renowned *The Forgotten People* radio address was number 20, given on 20 May 1942.

Menzies was all for rejecting class struggle, dividing the

nation into rich and poor and middle classes. He argued that the rich were able to look after themselves, while the poorer members of society were 'almost invariably well-organised, and with their wages and conditions safeguarded by popular law,' as they should be. He was concerned about those in the 'middle':

> *I do not believe that the real life of this nation is to be found either in great luxury hotels and the petty gossip of so-called fashionable suburbs, or in the officialdom of the organised masses.*
>
> *It is to be found in the homes of people who are nameless and unadvertised, and who, whatever their individual religious conviction or dogma, see in their children their greatest contribution to the immortality of their race.*
>
> *The home is the foundation of sanity and sobriety; it is the indispensable condition of continuity; its health determines the health of society as a whole.*

Was Menzies reading John Stuart Mill in preparation for his radio address?

> *The material home represents the concrete expression of the habits of frugality and saving for a home of our own. Your advanced socialist may rave against private property even while he acquires it; but one of the best instincts in us is that which induces us to have one little piece of earth with a house and a garden which is ours; to which we can*

> *withdraw, in which we can be among our friends,*
> *into which no stranger may come against our will.*

His defence of the 'materiality' of the home was followed by insistence on the 'humanity' of the home:

> *My home is where my wife and children are. The instinct to be with them is the great instinct of civilised man; the instinct to give them a chance in life - to make them not leaners but lifters - is a noble instinct. If Scotland has made a great contribution to the theory and practice of education, it is because of the tradition of Scottish homes.*

Menzies would found the Liberal Party in 1944, winning government in 1949 and retiring in 1966. Menzies regarded his contribution to Tertiary Education as one of his great achievements. Troy Bramston concurs:

> *In 1955-57, the budget allocated $12 million in grants to universities. By 1964-66, this figure had increased to $117 million. The number of universities doubled from six in 1949 to 12 by 1965. The facilities at universities, the resources they needed, and the quality of teaching and student performance had vastly improved since 1949 (Bramston, Robert Menzies: The Art of Politics (2019), 205).*

Henry Parkes would have been delighted. But did he 'turn in his grave' when the decision was made to increase government funding for private schools, including Catholic Schools, in 1963, precipitated by the famous Goulburn

School Strike in July 1962?

Home ownership increased from 53 per cent in the late 1940s to 71 per cent by the mid-1960s:

> *The number of weeks of work, at an average wage, required to purchase an Australian capital-city median-priced house declined sharply, from 301 in 1950 to 200 in 1955 (John Howard, The Menzies Era (2014), 372).*

Menzies disliked big government, but the 'last budget of the Menzies government to be in surplus was in 1952-53. The size of government expanded from 26.7 per cent of GDP in 1949 to 28.4 per cent by 1969' *(Bramston, Robert Menzies, 190)*.

Australian folklore has it that Liberal governments spend less than Labor governments, but it was the Hawke/Keating government, facing a terms of trade collapse in 1986-7, that reduced government spending from 26.9 per cent of GDP to 23.1 per cent in 1988-9.

Hawke and Keating (1983-1996) liberalised the Australian economy. The Whitlam government reduced tariffs by 25 per cent in 1973, attempting to reduce inflation. But the systematic liberalisation of the Australian economy was carried out by Hawke and Keating.

They floated the Australian dollar, giving the nation another 'natural mechanism' for enhanced international trade, but also being a 'thermometer' of economic health. The cumbersome centralised wage system was updated, continuing a just wage, but permitting enterprise bargaining in the labour market.

Two further 'natural mechanisms' were embedded in Australian life: a health system with a mix of public and private health, ensuring universal health coverage, and compulsory superannuation allowing average Australians to participate in the wealth of the nation.

Reform of gun laws by Prime Minister Howard and his deputy, Tim Fischer, after the Port Arthur massacre in 1996, was a significant contribution.

From Federation to now, we have benefited from stable, mostly competent governments, the legitimacy of which Australians have never challenged. If the peaceful and orderly transition from one government to another is symbolic of the heartbeat of a nation, then few palpitations have been felt.

Conclusion

By the turn of the 22nd Century will we still hold in our care a free and fair country? By then Australia's population is estimated to be approximately 65 million people.

Social harmony is facilitated when wealth is created and distributed justly, especially with respect to land and property. Challenges abound. In 1955, approximately 3.8 years of the annual wage were required to buy a median priced house in a capital city in Australia.

Almost 70 years on, what do we experience?

In 2022, Sydneysiders need 17.5 years of annual wage to buy a median priced house, Melbournians 12, people living in the city of Brisbane 9.2, residents of Canberra 12.4. The average for Australian capital cities is approximately 11 to 12 years of the annual wage needed to purchase a median priced house.

Is this what we want? Why do we now find ourselves in this precarious position? Can something be done?

Price is the result of an interplay between supply and demand. Identifying *self-interest* both in the public and private sector and focusing our attention on *public interest* is essential. This needs be an intentional and communal project, with the best of minds in political, public and private life engaged to 'put the cards on the table.' It must be a bipartisan project.

Why is supply constrained in a country like Australia? What benefits are State and Local Governments gaining from the present arrangements? What fiscal, tax and monetary policies need challenging and changing? Can the cost of building be lowered? It will take competence and courage.

Marriage rates are at historic lows and our marriages continue to break-up. As a consequence, families are under immense pressure, and yet, as observed in ancient and modern times, the family is the primary and most natural community and institution, enabling stability and humane advancement. Is it hindered or helped by government policy?

Not surprisingly our fertility rate has dropped to historic lows (1.6 births per woman in 2022). Our demographics are not as bad as China, Russia and other nations. Replacement rate is normally 2.1 births per woman, but China will need a rate far higher because of its endemic one child policy and practice of selective abortions of female babies. By the end of the 21st Century the Chinese population will be at least 20 per cent less than now, probably 50 per cent less, bearing in mind that official figures from the *People's Republic of China* are notoriously unreliable.

Demographers are now speaking of world *de-population*. As societies become more educated, birth rates recede. People marry later in life and have fewer children.

Longevity, too, must be impacting. If I am going to live to 85 or 90 years of age, why 'tie the knot' early?

The 'materialistic' world view holds sway and says 'another child is another mouth to feed.' In reality, however, it is the 'humanistic' view that is closer to the truth. 'Another child is another creative mind and set of hands,' an 'active potency,' a 'genius in waiting,' preparing to transform the world. Undoubtedly, a country's greatest resource is its people. Good demographics are fundamental to the health of a nation.

Gross Federal Government debt in 2022 is close on $1,000 billion (45.1% of GDP), trending towards $1,200 billion by 2027 (50% of GDP). An interest rate of 5% will see us pay more in debt repayments than we spend on *Medicare.*

Will debt suffocate us and hinder our attempts for a free and fair society? We have faced the challenge before. Joseph Lyons (1879-1939) presided over the repayment of large government debts during his time as Prime Minister (1932-39). Before World War II gross debt as a percentage of GDP was 40 per cent and rose to 120 per cent by 1945. The Howard government in 1996 turned a $96 billion net government debt into $29 billion of net financial assets by 2007.

The structural problem is manifest. In 2022 the ratio of Federal Government expenditure to GDP is 38.9%, expected to drop to 36% by 2027. A hearty appetite for reform will be needed by politicians, a deep resilience will be required from the Australian people.

Historian Geoff Blainey believes the last fifty years have witnessed one of the most fascinating intellectual and practical debates since the Industrial Revolution. Ecology and environment have risen dramatically in our consciousness. Concern for our common home is shared by all generations of Australians. We are rightly fascinated by 'working with nature rather than against it.' Climate change is one issue on the radar, but important environmental concerns such as the use of plastics and its effects on the natural world are perhaps more crucial.

The *Commonwealth Scientific and Industrial Research Organisation (CSIRO)* was established in 1926, initially set up by Prime Minister Billy Hughes in 1916 when it was known as the *Advisory Council of Science and Industry.* Continued and increased funding for research is a clear and ever-present need, but so too the development of more intimate ties to private enterprise and industry. Much will be achieved by governments having longer-term attitudes, rejecting the impulse to give in to 'rent-seeking' that has characterised much of our behaviour to date.

The Next Hundred Years

What social, economic, political and cultural *paradigm* do we have to enable continuance of a free and fair society? Is it possible to find common ground among the majority of Australians with a reasoned approach?

The Constitution of Australia establishes the fields of

policy and institutions to achieve such a society. Our history suggests that we should be optimistic as we journey deeper into the 21st Century.

From the initial migration to the country approximately 65,000 years ago, to the recent migration in 1788, from colonial times through Federation to the modern society that we now enjoy, much has been done, enabling us to live freely and fairly. Furthermore, we've been able to address those attitudes and practices that have contradicted and impeded our intent.

There is one recent piece of history that we have not yet considered. It has universal appeal to people of goodwill and can inform our approach. Chapter 1 presented its historical foundations, giving us a 'futuristic glimpse.'

Modern Catholic Social Teaching has undergone the most profound development since 1891. Successive popes have engaged in the social question with a deep degree of interest since that time, without exception. Importantly, they base their arguments on human reason – the 'natural light' that shines within each human person.

Kemp in his work notes the early defensiveness of the popes and the Catholic Church to the modern liberal and enlightened movement. This is not contested.

The suspicion of the Church was undoubtedly fuelled by the French Revolution and its attacks on religion, evocatively symbolised by the gaoling of Pope Pius VI by Napoleon in 1798. The pope was to die in gaol and his successor was imprisoned too, liberated in 1814. The experience was searing, setting in train a reactive response.

Pope Pius IX (1846-1878) was nicknamed *'Pio No No,'* a play on the pronunciation of his Italian name. He was a most strident critic of liberalism. He condemned the proposition:

> *That the Roman Pontiff can and should reconcile himself with progress, liberalism and modern civilisation.*

But the intransigence petered out. Upon his death, the next pope took the name Leo XIII. Elected in 1878, Leo was to be the first truly modern pope. It was he who published the first social encyclical (teaching) of the modern era. It was the first of many such documents and pronouncements by successive popes indicating dialogue with, not antagonism against, the modern world and its developments.

Leo's teaching document was called *Rerum Novarum,* the Latin name meaning *Of New Things.* It was published in 1891. In it he faced the changes brought about by the industrial revolution, the growing disparity of wealth, the issue of a just wage and the Marxist solution. In it he acknowledges the importance of a sound theory of the State, utilising legislative, executive and judicial power, demonstrating his modern proclivities. Cardinal Moran, third Catholic Archbishop of Sydney (1884-1911), strongly promoted Leo's social thought in Australia.

Surprisingly, his first move was to defend the right to

private property. He offered a practical and philosophical defence. The proposal to socialise property is 'so clearly futile for all practical purposes' that if it were implemented 'the working man himself would be among the first to suffer.' Then came the philosophical reasoning:

> *It is surely undeniable that, when a man engages in remunerative labour, the very reason and motive of his work is to obtain property, and to hold it as his own possession (Rerum Novarum, 4).*

Had Mill exerted his influence on the papacy? Reason undoubtedly guided the pope. Other observers note his reliance on the teaching of theologians in the preceding centuries of Christianity. The State, Leo says, has the duty to protect the 'sacred and inviolable' right to private property and the 'great labour question,' he insisted, cannot be solved without it.

Leo gives three reasons: property will be more equitably divided, greater wealth produced and national stability enhanced. At the same time he provided fiscal advice for the State:

> *These three important benefits, however, can only be expected on the condition that one's means be not drained and exhausted by excessive taxation. ... The State is, therefore, unjust and cruel, if in the name of taxation, it deprives the private owner of more than is just (Rerum Novarum, 35).*

Fast forward to 1931. Things had changed, but not got

easier. The Great Depression had well and truly begun, fascism and communism had become mass movements, liberal confidence shattered, democracy faltering.

Pope Pius XI (1922-1939) delivered his assessment with another teaching document, celebrating the fortieth anniversary of *Rerum Novarum*. He confirmed and renewed a fundamental principle of social philosophy, the *principle of subsidiarity:*

> *A community of a higher order should not interfere in the internal life of a community of a lower order, depriving the latter of its functions, but rather should support it.*

The principle has a threefold importance. The pope was concerned with the disappearance of a highly developed social life at the time. Individualism was on the rise in the West and was seemingly ascendant. Where were all those 'intermediary bodies' that are the fruit of personal and voluntary initiative, giving such vitality to society, creating rich and dynamic communities, all of which enriched human experience and human beings?

Second, the vacuum left was inevitably filled by the State, 'now encumbered with all burdens once borne by the disbanded associations.' Third, the principle is a defence and protection against socialism, against the wresting of private initiative away from the individual, transferring it to the State.

Subsidiarity issued a call for participation. Ordinary

citizens, through the arousal of their consciences, were being asked to involve themselves in the life of nations through intermediary bodies and communities, providing and supporting the rich tapestry of social life.

Within a forty year period, therefore, we have a strident defence of *private property* and *private initiative* in the social sphere.

The great symbol of communism and the division between it and the free world, the *Berlin Wall,* collapsed in 1989. Pope John Paul II was elected pope in 1978, the first non-Italian pope for over 400 years, one who had experienced fascism and communism first hand.

In 1991 he commemorated the one hundredth anniversary of *Rerum Novarum* with his own powerful teaching document. It was called *Centesimus Annus,* Latin for *One Hundred Years.*

John Paul II was steeped in the philosophical and theological approach of St. Thomas Aquinas and a new philosophy called *Phenomenology.* The latter is a body of thought showing particular sensitivity to human experience and how persons, events and things are manifest through such experience.

He built on the teaching of Leo XIII and Pius XI and acknowledged the importance of private property and private initiative in the social development of nations. In particular, he focused on the freedom of the human person:

> *Experience shows us that the denial of this right,*

or its limitation in the name of an alleged 'equality' of everyone in society, diminishes, or in practice absolutely destroys the spirit of initiative, that is to say the creative subjectivity of the citizen.

As a consequence, there arises, not so much a true equality as a 'levelling down.' In the place of creative initiative there appears passivity, dependence and submission to the bureaucratic apparatus.

Reasonably, the right to private property and private initiative is not absolute, since it is orientated towards the *common good*. One has the *right* to possess material things, but one has the *responsibility* to make them available to those who would benefit from their use. The distinction between *possession* and *use* is understood to be foundational to a free and fair society.

As a consequence of this personal and social philosophical principle, Pope John Paul II coined the statement, *'All private property has a social mortgage on it.'*

Perhaps the family home is the best example. A house purchased by a young couple for their life together is made available to their children, extended family, etc.

After the disastrous experience of communism (1917-1989), with all its abject poverty, and the mixed experience of some capitalistic economies tending towards *laissez faire,* John Paul II called for a society of *free work, enterprise and participation,* with the state and culture combining to provide a framework for freedom and fairness.

The 'Paradigm'

There have been 16 social teaching documents since 1891. The legacy is significant and not sectarian. The documents are at their best when articulating social principles, not so much when advocating specific solutions, which are best left to the experts in each field of human endeavour.

From this rich, recent historical development in Catholic Social thought, it is possible to articulate the following paradigm with *four foundational principles,* aiding free and fair societies. The paradigm is a *subsiduum* – an *aid:*

> *The dignity and freedom of the human person*
>
> *The common good*
>
> *The principle of subsidiarity*
>
> *The principle of solidarity.*

The central tenet of the paradigm is that 'individual human beings are the *foundation,* the *cause* and the *end* of every social institution'. This is a constant mantra over the 130 year history of modern social teaching and indeed from the onset of Christian social engagement.

The human person is understood to be *body, soul and spirit*, made in the image and likeness of God, giving rise to certain inalienable rights and responsibilities. Human dignity is to be pursued relentlessly and defended vigorously with no exceptions, otherwise we reap injustice.

The *common good* is a term largely forgotten in our

parlance. It needs rehabilitation and re-formulation.

It is defined as all those *conditions* in society that enable human beings to survive and thrive. Think life itself, food, health, education, leisure, housing, the rule of law, state bodies, intermediary bodies, marriage, family, employment, just wage, etc.

Defence and promotion of the *common good* ensures that *self-interest* becomes *public-interest,* defending us against the pitting of one minority group against or in favour of another.

The principle of *solidarity* and the principle of *subsidiarity* are intimately related, mutually informing one another.

The principle of subsidiarity echoes in the lives of individuals, calling them to participate in the life of the nation, especially in the vast array of communal groupings that lie between individual persons and government.

We are personal and social beings able to achieve little by solitary activity. Hence, the principle of solidarity, working *with* and *for* others. The well-known *Parable of the Good Samaritan* informs, as do the symbolic lives of Francis of Assisi and Mother Teresa of Calcutta. We see in the other a 'sister,' a 'brother.'

The paradigm is not prescriptive, can be applied in various ways, but is seamless. Forgo one of the principles and the others wither on the vine.

History is our witness. When the paradigm has been

honoured, we have done well. When it has been forgotten, annulled or trashed, we haven't.

As the 21st Century unfolds, we do well to humbly rely on each other and 'on the blessing of Almighty God' as the preamble to the Constitution states. Experience teaches that 'most of life depends upon the company we keep.' Relying on human and divine company is not a sign of weakness, but wisdom.

The symbolism of the Australian Flag should not be ignored either. It encourages us to 'look forward to success, enabled by looking upward for support.'

Undoubtedly, we are living not in an 'era of change, but a change of era.' We face many challenges, but vast opportunities lie before us.

Our desire for a free and fair country continues to be realistic and achievable, but only if we continue to reverence fundamental human values.

Epilogue

I had originally thought that the monograph should be called, *'Australia: What went right?'*

But then the sabbatical time permitted a lot of reading and research and so *'What went wrong?'* had to be added.

For some reason, psychologists have observed that people place a lot more weight on what goes wrong than on what goes right.

Why, I wonder?

At any rate, I do hope that this brief monograph will inspire many young people to enter into public and political life.

That's what happened in the past. It's the reason why Australia is so good.

It needs to happen again.

www.ingramcontent.com/pod-product-compliance
Lightning Source LLC
Chambersburg PA
CBHW021946160426
43195CB00011B/1236